CH00922294

Forestry Comm

Handbook 8

Establishing Farm Woodlands

An account of experimental work
which has taken place
on ADAS Research and Development
Farms and on private land in conjunction
with Willmot Industries
Conservation Department
and Tilhill Economic Forestry.

By D.R. Williamson
Silviculturist,
Forestry Commission

LONDON: HMSO

ISBN 0 11 710309 8

FDC 232.4 : 26 : 913 : (410)

Keywords: Establishment, Farm woodlands, Forestry

British Library Cataloguing in Publication Data
A CIP catalogue record for this book is available from the British Library

HMSO publications are available from:

HMSO Publications Centre
(Mail, fax and telephone orders only)
PO Box 276, London, SW8 5DT
Telephone orders 071–873 9090
General enquiries 071–873 0011
(queuing system in operation for both numbers)
Fax orders 071–873 8200

HMSO Bookshops
49 High Holborn, London, WC1V 6HB
(counter service only)
071–873 0011 Fax 071–873 8200
258 Broad Street, Birmingham, B1 2HE
021–643 3740 Fax 021–643 6510
Southey House, 33 Wine Street, Bristol, BS1 2BQ
0272 264306 Fax 0272 294515
9-21 Princess Street, Manchester, M60 8AS
061–834 7201 Fax 061–833 0634
16 Arthur Street, Belfast, BT1 4GD
0232 238451 Fax 0232 235401
71 Lothian Road, Edinburgh, EH3 9AZ
031–228 4181 Fax 031–229 2734

HMSO's Accredited Agents
(see Yellow Pages)

and through good booksellers

Acknowledgements

The information contained within this publication has been gathered through an association with various organisations. The inspiration for the work on ground flora management on fertile arable sites came largely from Marek Nowakowski of Willmot Industries Conservation Department. I also wish to express my thanks to the managers and staff of the ADAS Research and Development Farms where many of the experiments which support this text were sited. Gratitude is also owed to David Clay, Dick Makepeace, Gary Kerr, Richard Ferris-Kaan, Derek Nelson, Chris Nixon, Paul Tabbush and Julian Evans for comments and contributions to this text. I am truly indebted to my Forest Officer and industrial staff colleagues within the Forestry Commission without whom the farm woodland experimental programme would not have been possible. Additionally I would like to thank Mr and Mrs A. Hichens for providing arable land for farm woodland experiments, and Roger Boswell and Tracy Houston who have been responsible for overseeing design and undertaking statistical analysis of the farm woodland experiments.

Front cover
Upper right Planting a farm woodland establishment trial.

Lower right Careful handling of planting stock between lifting in the nursery and planting out is essential. The use of co-extruded polythene bags reduces the risk of stock plants overheating and the roots drying out.

Lower left Farm woodland established with the use of treeshelters and with effective weed control along the planted rows. The inter-row is sown with a grass/wildflower mixture which prevents the prolific growth of weeds and provides an attractive feature with considerable wildlife benefits.

Upper left Wild cherry established in treeshelters, with kale as an inter-row game cover.

Contents

Establishing Farm Woodlands

Etablissement de Forêts sur des Terres Arables

Summary

Results from the first Forestry Commission experiments set up to examine the establishment of trees on ex-agricultural land in the lowlands revealed that the methods developed for tree planting in the uplands were not wholly transferable. The planting and establishment of trees on land that had previously been under an arable rotation proved to be particularly challenging.

This Handbook contains practical guidance based on experience gained during 3 years of tree establishment trials on farms throughout southern England. The text describes the site preparation that should be undertaken, then emphasises the importance of controlling weeds around the base of trees and managing the vegetation between the weed-free areas. Various techniques for utilising the inter-row strips are suggested, to enable the farmer to achieve objectives such as game cover and habitat creation, in addition to successful tree establishment.

Résumé

Les résultats des premières expériences menées par la Forestry Commission dans le but d'étudier la plantation d'arbres sur d'anciennes terres agricoles situées en basses plaines ont révélé que les méthodes de plantation utilisées sur les hauts plateaux ne sont pas totalement applicables. Le développement des arbres plantés sur des terres jusqu'alors consacrées à la rotation des cultures s'avère particulièrement difficile.

Ce livret contient des conseils pratiques basés sur trois années d'expérience consacrées à des essais de plantation d'arbres dans tout le sud de l'Angleterre. Il décrit la préparation du terrain, met l'accent sur la nécessité de contrôler les mauvaises herbes à la base des arbres et la végétation qui pousse entre les arbres. Différentes méthodes sont suggérées pour utiliser l'espace entre les rangées d'arbres, afin de permettre à l'agriculteur de favoriser la création d'un habitat et de nombreux abris pour le gibier, tout en garantissant une croissance réussie des arbres.

Das Anlegen von Bauernwäldern

Zusammenfassung

Die Ergebnisse der ersten forstbehördlichen Experimente zur Untersuchung des Anbaues von Bäumen auf ehemalig landwirtschaftlich genutztem Land im Tiefland zeigten, daß sich die Methoden, die zur Baumpflanzung im Hochland entwickelt wurden, nicht immer übertragen lassen. Die Pflanzung und Weiterpflege von Bäumen auf Land das vorher unter einem Fruchtwechselsystem bewirtschaftet wurde erwieß sich als besonders beanspruchend.

Dieses Handbuch enthält praktische Anleitungen die sich auf Erfahrungen stützen, die über einen Zeitraum von 3 Jahren in Anbauversuchen auf Gütern in Südengland gesammelt wurden. Der Text beschreibt die Standorfvorbereitung die unternommen werden sollte, dann wird die Bedeutung der Unkrautbekämpfung im Bereich des Baumstammes und die Kontrolle der Vegetation zwischen den unkrautfreien Bereichen unterstrichen. Verschiedene Techniken zur Nutzung der Bereiche zwischen den Pflanzreihen werden vorgeschlagen, um es dem Landwirt zu ermöglichen, neben dem erfolgreichem Anbau von Bäumen auch andere Ziele, wie z.B. Deckung und Standortschaffung für Wild, zu verwirklichen.

1   Tree planting opportunities on farms

Introduction

Farmers are now faced with surpluses and falling incomes and as a result they and landowners in general are being encouraged to diversify into new land use activities. Woodland is one of the options which many farmers are considering. Britain only produces about 12% of its industrial timber requirements and this results in an import bill for timber and timber products in excess of £7 billion every year. There is therefore little doubt that British grown timber will continue to be in high demand. Moreover only 10% of Britain has woodland cover, which is one of the lowest proportions in Europe. New woodland brings added landscape, conservation, amenity and sporting interest to farms.

There are several grant schemes available to encourage landowners and farmers to plant trees and woodland. These allow a wide range of objectives to be satisfied through tree planting. Full details of the grants that are available can be obtained from your local Forestry Authority office.

An opportunity exists to create a beautiful and functional countryside through tree planting, but this can only be achieved if farmers have access to practical and cost-effective techniques for establishing and managing trees. The Forestry Commission's Research Division has been addressing these issues with on-farm experiments including some on ADAS Research and Development Farms, and is now able to make recommendations for the establishment of woodland on ex-agricultural land.

Woodland options when planting trees on fertile farmland

The Forestry Commission has been engaged in afforestation since its formation in 1919 and success-

PLATE 1   Arable energy coppice planted at close spacing to achieve maximum yield over a short rotation. (38623)

1

ful methods for establishing trees on infertile upland sites have been proven through a sustained research and development programme. Unfortunately the methods that work well in the uplands are not wholly transferable to tree establishment on fertile lowland sites where many of the conditions are different.

When a farmer or landowner is considering planting trees on agricultural land he has a number of options:

- **Woodlands grown to maturity.** These are areas planted with a range of woodland tree species which will be expected to remain in place for a long period of time. They will be expected to produce traditional woodland products and have a high wildlife, sporting and amenity value.
- **Short rotation coppice.** This can be sub-divided as follows:

  Traditional coppice. These areas are planted with broadleaved species, often in stands of a single species to produce small diameter material for a specific market. Such areas are usually managed on rotations of greater than 10 years. There is the option to allow some coppiced trees to grow on to form a woodland canopy under a coppice with standards system.

  Arable energy crops. These are crops which utilise fast growing broadleaved species planted at close spacings specifically to produce combustible wood chips for the energy generation market. Such areas are usually managed on coppice rotations of 1–4 years.

  Agro-forestry. Widely spaced trees, planted to allow intercropping with an arable crop or grazing animals.

This publication is aimed at helping those planning the establishment of farm woodlands on fertile sites, but much of the information is equally relevant to the establishment of short rotation coppice and agro-forestry systems.

The scope of this publication

This Handbook is a practical guide on how to establish trees and woodlands successfully on fertile land that has been under agricultural management; whether improved grassland or arable cropping. Most of the experimental work which forms the background to this publication has taken place in the drier southern counties of Britain but many of the principles also apply to lowland areas in the wetter western and northern parts of the British Isles.

PLATE 2 Traditional coppice with widely spaced stools. (38176)

2 Where to plant and why

Objectives of woodland creation and management

There are several reasons for planting trees, the most obvious being to produce timber. However, trees and woodlands, including those that are planted with timber production in mind, can provide many other benefits such as landscape enhancement, shelter, opportunities for recreation and the creation of habitats for game and other animals and plants. When undertaking new planting many additional objectives can be accommodated through management of the inter-row (the space between the trees) and conservation projects or game cover crops are just two examples of how this area can be used.

Even where woodlands are planted with the specific aim of producing income it will be some time before they provide revenue through timber sales. In the early years of establishment, generating income from other products such as foliage and flowers for florists, Christmas trees and even free range poultry may be considered.

Improving the visual appearance of the farm and so possibly enhancing its capital value is often seen as important but this can be achieved along with other more specific aims.

The current grant schemes give applicants the widest possible choice in the way they create and manage their new woodlands. However, multiple objectives demand compromise. Even within a single broad objective, such as increasing species diversity, it is important that the parameters are sufficiently well defined, otherwise difficulties may arise because by treating the area to favour one type of plant or animal another group may be disadvantaged.

The setting of objectives becomes even more important if the woodland is to be managed by a number of individuals or organisations each with particular interests. Management will be easier in the long term if careful thought is given to the details of the scheme before planting.

Farm woodland establishment: where to plant

In many cases the actual location on the farm to be planted with trees will already have been determined. Typical areas include:

- low productivity land;
- awkward shaped fields, parts of fields or steep ground;
- land adjacent to existing woodlands;
- land adjacent to ponds, tracks, buildings and other features.

When such areas have been identified, the objectives to be satisfied by the planting scheme will need to be tailored to suit the particular piece of ground.

In other cases farmers will have firm ideas of what they require from an area of woodland and a survey of the farm will reveal the optimum site for this chosen purpose. This will not always be on marginal ground and it is therefore likely that better quality land will be planted with trees when this approach is taken. For example, there may be an area of the farm where trees are required to screen a building or provide shelter. Game shooting is an important enterprise on many farms and a good shoot can only be created or improved through the correct planning and siting of game spinnies. In the same way an area of the farm may provide a particular conservation opportunity that can be improved through woodland creation.

Regardless of the main purpose of tree planting, the effect on the landscape must be considered. Trees and woodland are prominent features in any landscape and are often seen by many generations. The main factors affecting the landscape value of woodland are size, shape, species choice and structure. The size and shape of a woodland should be in scale with the local landform and landscape. In large scale, open country with far reaching views, large blocks of woodland are appropriate, but in small scale landscapes where only small sections of the countryside can be seen from one view point small woodlands are more applicable.

3 Soil and site factors affecting establishment of woodland on fertile agricultural sites

Site differences

In many respects the establishment of woodlands on fertile farmland would appear to be an easier task than that faced by the upland forester with exposed sites, poor soils and rough terrain. From the forester's point of view the prospect of access to fertile lowland ground is exciting because at first sight it appears that a wide range of tree species can be used and rapid growth rates achieved.

However, there are important differences between tree establishment in the uplands and on fertile farmland, and although many are obvious they must be recognised and planned for to achieve success.

Accessibility

To farm efficiently lowland farmers have invested heavily in mechanisation. As a result the labour force on most farms is small in relation to the area farmed and there is often not the surplus manpower to carry out forestry tasks, particularly at the times of the year when agricultural operations are at a peak. For this reason many farmers will want to mechanise the maintenance of their farm woodlands as far as possible.

Agricultural fields in the lowlands are usually accessible in terms of terrain and distance from a road or track but there are often intensively managed, high value arable crops surrounding potential planting sites. If this is the case it may render the site inaccessible to all but pedestrian traffic for most of the growing season. Serious consideration must therefore be given to the accessibility of sites especially if it is planned to mechanise maintenance operations.

Previous land use

The previous land use of a planting site is an important factor determining the treatment of the site before and after planting.

There are basically two starting points when establishing a lowland farm woodland: a grass sward and an arable stubble.

Planting into a grass sward

A grass sward is the simplest starting point. Unless the soil has been badly compacted by stock or heavy machinery the *grass sward should not be disturbed*. It is best to plant through the sward and then control the grass around the trees with a suitable herbicide applied post-planting as a spot or strip treatment. The remaining grass can either be left to grow rank and provide a wildlife habitat or it can be mown as required. Killing the sward over the whole site with

PLATE 3 When planting trees into grass do not disturb the sward but plant through it and control the grass around the tree with a suitable herbicide post-planting.

herbicides or thorough cultivation will create an ideal site for the invasion of arable weeds; these will be more difficult and more expensive to manage than grass. Unmanaged weeds may act as a seed source to contaminate neighbouring fields.

Cultivation of a grass sward should only be undertaken if the establishment of a different inter-row vegetation is being considered to achieve objectives in addition to tree establishment (see 'Weed and vegetation management' pp.25–38) or trees are being planted at very close spacing, e.g. for arable energy coppice. Cultivation in the form of mounds or raised ridges may also be beneficial on marginal sites in areas of high rainfall to avoid waterlogging.

If the soil is compacted this should be ameliorated by ripping. The ripping operation can be organised to provide an easy planting site with the tree planting lines marked and the planting slot already cre-

ated. However, when planting trees into heavy textured soils do not be tempted to plant in the rip lines. In dry seasons the soil will shrink and the rip line can open exposing the roots of the newly planted trees, leading to instability and high mortality (see 'Soil type' pp.10–12). On extremely heavy land the ripping operation should be organised so that trees are planted midway between two rip lines.

Planting into an arable stubble

The most important decision when faced with an arable stubble is whether to plough before planting. On sites with a light soil trees should be planted directly into the undisturbed stubble, although it may be better to wait until the soil has been rewetted by autumn rains. This delay is not usually a problem because planting is not normally carried out until dormant trees are available from the nursery. The use of herbicides during the management of the previous arable crop will reduce the quantity of viable weed seeds in the surface layer of the soil. Leaving the arable stubble undisturbed may therefore delay the invasion of annual broadleaved weeds, although there may be rapid germination of weed grasses and volunteers. If the site is compacted then ripping will be necessary (see 'Planting into a grass sward').

On sites with heavy soils the situation is more difficult. When the ground is dry following a summer with low rainfall it is difficult, if not impossible, to plant directly into a stubble. Even if a planting hole/notch can be created the soil will not crumble and cannot be gently firmed around the tree roots. There are several options regarding site treatment before planting and the decision on which one to choose depends on the season and the individual circumstances associated with the particular site.

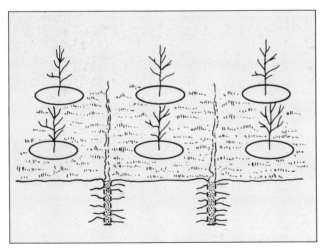

FIGURE 1 When soil compaction has to be ameliorated by ripping do not plant in the rip lines. In dry seasons, particularly on heavy land, the soil will shrink and the rip lines can open, exposing roots of newly planted trees which leads to high mortality.

- Leave until the weather (rainfall) has made the site more manageable and plant directly into the stubble.
- Cultivate narrow strips or the whole site if inter-row vegetation is to be established (see 'Weed and vegetation management' pp.25–38). On heavy soils there is often only a brief period in the autumn when conditions allow cultivation to take place without damage to the soil structure. Manual planting can take place even when the prevailing conditions do not allow the use of machinery, but it can be a difficult and unpleasant task if done when the soil is wet. Large clods of soil can stick to the planting spade and to boots making the job slow and tiring, and the sides of the planting hole or notch will be smeared slowing or preventing root development of the trees. The smeared sides of the planting hole/notch also remain as a line of weakness in the soil and as the soil dries in the summer it can crack along this line exposing the tree roots and causing losses.

If, before the last arable crop is sown, an area of the farm which is under an arable rotation is earmarked for tree planting then a number of options are available to facilitate tree establishment, given favourable soil conditions.

Planting into a grass sward is the simplest and cheapest starting point for a farm woodland, therefore if an arable crop is selected, which allows the undersowing of a low productivity grass sward, this can be in place by the time of tree planting. Of course this will only be a viable option if it fits in with the main farm enterprise.

Where a cereal crop (which is not undersown) is grown before a farm woodland is planted the straw can be chopped and left on site. This will help to conserve soil moisture (see 'Soil type') and reduce weed growth by acting as a mulch.

PLATE 4 The smeared sides of a planting notch remain as a line of weakness in the soil. As the soil dries it cracks along this line exposing tree roots.

Soil type: physical properties

When arable land is taken out of production and planted with trees it is often the areas that give a marginal financial return or are not suited to modern farming techniques that are planted first. Many such sites have heavy clay soils with poor soil structure due to annual cultivation.

These heavy textured soils require special attention. When wetted by autumn rains the soil particles swell, closing soil fissures and preventing further drainage. The soil remains waterlogged through the winter until it starts to dry in the spring. As the soil dries it shrinks causing cracking, a process often aided by frost. This promotes natural drainage and allows air to enter the soil which in turn speeds the drying process leading to further cracking. The result is that the water-table falls quickly in the spring and in dry seasons heavy textured soils can be prone to drought.

Initially it is difficult to manage perennial crops on such sites. When establishing farm woodlands on heavy clays careful consideration must be given to any proposed action because the management of the soil and the ground vegetation are inter-related, i.e. treating the site to relieve one set of conditions, such as waterlogging, will probably make the effect of summer drought worse.

The following problems may be encountered when planting trees on heavy clay soil.

1. **Waterlogging.** Physical drainage is poor on these sites, but the creation of ridges to elevate the planting position is counter-productive as it promotes drought in summer. The establishment of ground vegetation in the inter-row may aid the removal of water from the soil by transpiration and grass roots will help to promote good soil structure, and hence better drainage. But vegetation and particularly grass will compete strongly for moisture in the summer and may also increase soil cracking in the tree rows during the summer (see 'Soil shrink–swell potential' below) with the result of hindering tree rooting and the stability of young trees.

2. **Soil moisture deficit.** Ground disturbance by cultivation appears to promote soil moisture deficit and minimum ground preparation is probably the best way to conserve soil moisture on heavy clay sites (see 'Previous land use' pp.6–9). Attention to weed control will reduce competition for water between the trees and the ground vegetation, and mulch mats may have an additional role in water conservation.

3. **Soil shrink–swell potential.** Clay soils shrink more than light textured soils and are therefore prone to crack to a greater extent. Cracks will occur on all sites except where the soil is kept completely bare of ground vegetation. Vigorous vegetation dries the soil which shrinks and cracks.

   Where ground vegetation grows uniformly over the whole site the soil is dried evenly and although the area will be covered in a network of cracks they will be small and randomly distributed. On such sites where spot weeding takes place the soil may crack around the circumference of the spot. However, only on the heaviest soils, in dry seasons, will there be serious tree losses due to shrinkage cracks running through the planting hole/notch.

   But where uneven shrinkage is promoted, e.g. in plantations where strip weeding takes place in a grass sward, the soil cracks will be large and concentrated along lines of weakness in the soil, usually along the centre of the weed free strip.

PLATE 5 On heavy land in dry seasons where strip weeding takes place in vigorous ground vegetation, uneven soil shrinkage is promoted. The soil cracking is concentrated in the weed-free strip. (*Willmot Industries*)

On the heaviest clays the best solution may be to keep the soil more or less bare until the trees are established and then cultivate the inter-row and sow a desirable ground cover crop. Alternatively, the adverse effects of uneven soil shrinkage may be ameliorated by ripping in late spring on either side of the weed free strip to isolate the weed free area from the grass sward, but this technique remains experimental.

Soil biology

Maintaining a cover of vegetation between the trees will encourage earthworm activity and so aid structural development and drainage of the soil through burrowing activity and the incorporation of organic matter.

Soil pH

Many agricultural soils, even those which are not naturally calcareous, have a higher pH than most forest soils. The optimum pH for most agricultural crops (particularly arable crops) is pH 6.5 and for this reason land under agricultural management is usually heavily limed. Where this has raised the pH above 7 many tree species will not survive, though there are exceptions (see Table 1). It is therefore essential to carry out a soil test to establish the pH of the site before tree planting. It is uneconomic and impracticable to consider reducing soil pH (e.g. with gypsum) so that a wider range of tree species can be grown. High pH is likely to inhibit the activity of the mycorrhizal fungi which are associated with tree roots and which aid tree nutrition, as these are usually found in more acid soils. There is little likelihood that mycorrhiza can be manipulated artificially so selection of a suitable tree species becomes important.

Soil fertility

Most agricultural sites, especially intensively farmed areas, have high fertility compared with traditional forest sites in the uplands. This fertility may persist for many years after agricultural cropping has ceased. However there are exceptions; on some freely drained sites where soil organic matter is low the nitrogen can be leached out of the soil and reduced to very low levels after as little as 2 years. Also soils with a high pH can lock up phosphorus making it unavailable to trees. Where these problems occur, deficiencies can be remedied using fertilisers (urea and superphosphate). There may be a role for using sewage sludge to amend infertility, but this can result in anaerobic conditions on heavier soils and on these sites artificial fertilisers are favoured.

4 Management of farm woodlands during the establishment period

Species choice

If a tree planting scheme is to be successful then species that match the characteristics of the site must be chosen. The most important features of any site are soil, climate and topography. The main soil types found on farms and the tree species that will grow on them are listed in Table 1. The major climatic and topographic influences on species choice are rainfall, altitude and exposure, frost and winter cold. In general, as altitude increases the rate of tree growth decreases. Exposure has the same effect and this can be seen on the edges of existing woodlands where the trees are shorter and more heavily branched. Rainfall has little effect on the choice of broadleaved species but a considerable effect on conifers. In general Corsican pine should not be planted in the wetter upland areas of the north and west due to the increased chance of disease (dieback caused by the fungus *Brunchorstia pinea*) but it grows well in the drier eastern counties. In contrast spruces should not be planted in low rainfall areas. Summer warmth is important for some species, notably sweet chestnut and poplar which grow better in southern Britain. Spring frosts can be a problem in the early years particularly of species which flush early in the year. Only when a list of species which are suited to the site has been drawn up can the species which best suit the objectives of tree planting be selected.

One of the early decisions will concern whether the new woodland should be made up of conifer or broadleaved trees, or a mixture. This will depend on the area in which the planting is taking place and on the objectives of management. A pure conifer planting may look out of place in the southern lowlands of England but may look very attractive on the lower slopes of an upland valley. A new planting containing both coniferous and broadleaved trees can often be advantageous when producing quality timber or providing shelter. Mixed woodlands are also valuable for wildlife and game. If shelter or shooting is the main reason for tree planting then a woodland containing both conifers and broadleaves will give most benefit.

The main consideration when establishing a woodland for game birds is the quantity and quality of woodland edge. Pheasants are primarily ground living birds and they select areas rich in low shrubby growth that provides warmth and shelter from predators. In new plantings the design and choice of species to plant along the edge is therefore particularly important. Privet, holly, yew, whitebeam, crab apple, hawthorn, willow, hazel, birch (*Betula pendula* for the north and west, *Betula pubescens* for the south), laurel and field maple (for southern Britain) and mountain ash all provide good cover from which to build a gradually sloping woodland edge. Other, non-native species such as *Cotoneater*, *Lonicera japonica* and snowberry may also be used but these are invasive and will almost certainly cause problems unless carefully managed.

13

If timber production is one of the main aims then the majority of the trees should be capable of producing high quality timber. With broadleaved trees this would include oak, beech, ash, wild cherry, sycamore, sweet chestnut, Norway maple and poplar. The major conifer species include Scots and Corsican pine, Norway and Sitka spruce, larch, and Douglas fir.

The tree species to be used in a woodland where the provision of wildlife habitat is of primary importance will depend on the species to be encouraged but will usually include a high proportion of native species that occur locally. When deciding what to plant a good starting point is to observe which tree species are growing well in the locality on similar sites.

Mixtures

In many areas of Britain it has been traditional to plant broadleaves in mixture with conifers. There are many advantages from using mixtures but management is more difficult. The fast growing conifers provide early revenue and on frosty sites can nurse the broadleaved species through the establishment phase. On most sites the growth of broadleaves in mixture with conifers is superior to that of a pure crop and through the 'nursing' effect the broadleaved trees are straighter and have fewer, smaller side branches.

Mixtures between broadleaved species which mature at different ages can also be successful. It is important to ensure that the species are compatible (have approximately similar height growth) and that all species are established satisfactorily. If mixtures are not compatible one species will tend to dominate, often suppressing the other, negating any physical and consequently any financial gain.

In undulating country mixtures of conifers and broadleaves planted in lines containing a single

PLATE 6 Bare-rooted oak produced in an open grown nursery. (40276). Plates 6–8; see 'Plant type' pp.16–18.

species can produce an ugly striped appearance. One solution is to plant groups of broadleaves in a matrix of conifers. For simplicity and robustness of the mixture it is sensible only to grow two species. For oak and beech a block and matrix layout of groups of

PLATE 7 Container grown oak. (40273)

PLATE 8 When container grown stock are removed from the container they are described as plugs. (40274)

12 or 16 broadleaved trees at 10–12 m centres is effective. With row mixtures it is preferable either to plant each species in bands of four or five rows wide, or in order to maximise conifer yield, to limit broadleaves to three row strips alternating with five or six rows of conifers. Each of these designs ensures that the broadleaved groups or strips are separated at about final crop spacing while allowing straightforward harvesting of the conifers.

Where compatible mixtures are to be grown, the following are found to work reasonably well, always provided the site is suitable in the first place:

Ash with: European larch and occasionally Norway spruce.

Beech with: Lawson cypress, western red cedar, Scots or Corsican pine and occasionally with European larch and Norway spruce.

Oak with: European larch, Norway spruce or Scots pine.

If planned properly the planting of mixtures can often have considerable landscape and wildlife advantages.

15

Table 1	Species recommendations for the major farm woodland site types					
	Brown earths Fen peats pH 4–7	Non-calcareous clay pH < 7	Calcareous clays pH ≥ 7	Alluvial soils pH 4–7	Shallow soils over chalk and limestone pH ≥ 7	Acidic sands and podzols pH < 4
Drainage	Good	Poor (winter waterlogging possible)		Poor – high water table	Good	Good
Fertility	High	Medium-high	Medium-high	High	Medium	Low
Special problems	None	Cracking in dry weather Severe on southern sites – less severe in north and west		Seasonal flooding	Rooting depth restrictions Lime-induced chlorosis	Ironpan on podzols Water deficits
Principal tree species for timber production	Oak Lime Ash Poplar Wild cherry Sycamore Beech Sweet chestnut Douglas fir Larches Corsican pine Norway spruce Western hemlock	Poplars Oak Ash Cherry Alder Willow Lime Beech Corsican pine Western red cedar Norway spruce Sitka spruce	Some poplars* Oak Ash Cherry Alder Willow Lime Corsican pine Western red cedar	Poplar Willow Alder Sitka spruce Norway spruce	Lime Italian alder Sycamore Norway maple Corsican pine Western red cedar Lawson cypress	Sweet chestnut Birch Scots pine Corsican pine Larches

* Not balsam poplars or balsam hybrids.

Plant type

Trees are sold in a wide variety of sizes and types, and at a range of prices. It is important that the correct and most cost-effective specifications are selected to suit the site to be planted. When buying any nursery stock always try to view the plants in the nursery during the growing season and look for stout, well balanced and healthy plants. Small (i.e. 20–40 cm) stock plants are cheaper to buy and replace. They are also easier to handle, store and plant and will survive better than larger stock types. Do ensure that trees are alive and healthy on receipt.

Check all bags and trays of plants, any suspect plants can be examined further by nicking the bark with a thumbnail: if green or greenish-white it is alive; if creamy-white or brown it is dead or dying.

Bare-rooted trees

These are sold as either transplants or undercuts. Transplants are produced by growing seedlings in a seedbed for 1–2 years before they are lifted and transplanted to grow on for another 1–2 years. This practice encourages a bushy root system on a well-balanced plant which has a good root:shoot ratio. This is vital because the root system must be able to provide all the needs of the shoot during the testing first season. The age of the plant and the regime under which it has been grown is given in nursery catalogues. A tree which spent 1 year in a seedbed and was then lifted and spent a further 1 year in a transplant line is described as a 1 + 1 plant.

Increasingly, open grown forest nursery stock are being produced as undercuts as it has been found that many species establish better following this regime in the nursery. This involves the seed being sown at lower density in the seed bed, usually in lines through a precision sower. The plants remain in the seedbed being undercut periodically, using a sharp reciprocating blade, to produce a compact and fibrous root system and a well balanced plant. Modern nursery techniques allow undercut stock of many species to be grown in one season and such stock are described as 1/2 u 1/2.

Container grown trees

This term refers to plants that have been grown in containers filled with an artificial growing medium which remains around the roots when planted out. It can cover a wide range of plant types from small pot and cell grown stock up to large heavy standards in huge containers. It is the smaller stock types which are used for farm woodland establishment.

A wide variety of containers are used but they can be divided into two broad categories, re-usable containers and Japanese paper pots (JPPs). The re-usable containers are usually moulded from plastic or polystyrene and the trees are removed from the containers before planting. When container grown stock are sold without the container they are described as plugs.

With JPP stock the container, which is made of tough paper, is planted with the tree and degrades over a period of time, although this can be many years on some sites. Container grown stock are usually sown under polythene tunnels where they remain for part of the growing season before being 'hardened off', often outside. This type of stock for woodland planting is usually produced in one growing season.

When container grown trees are transported to the planting site in the container they have the advantage that their roots are not exposed and they are less likely to be damaged during lifting, transport, and storage and may have a better chance of survival in certain conditions. The disadvantage is that where the ground being planted is very different in character from the growing compost, the roots can be slow to penetrate the surrounding soil. This frequently occurs on heavy clays.

Cuttings and rooted sets

Some species such as poplar and willow, root easily from cuttings. Therefore these species are usually established using unrooted (20–25 cm long; 1–2 cm diameter) cuttings which are simply inserted into the soil on suitable sites. The same species can be planted as rooted sets and while these will be more expensive to buy and plant they will give an early growth advantage, particularly on difficult sites.

Plant handling

The failure of trees to produce active shoot growth (flush) in the spring following planting, which usually results in trees dying early in the first growing season, can frequently be avoided if care is taken over the handling of plants from the time they leave the nursery to the time they are planted. The damage to be avoided tends to occur in three main ways:

Root drying

Even on dull, cool days a drying wind can quickly desiccate the root system of a young tree. Bare-rooted trees are therefore normally handled using special co-extruded black and white plastic bags. These bags, which are black on the inside and white on the outside are opaque, reflect the suns heat, and so keep trees cool inside. Plants should be sealed in such bags during storage. When planting, use a planting bag to keep the root moist until planting. Remove trees one at a time to avoid desiccation. Old fertiliser bags are not suitable as any chemical remains will scorch the roots of young trees.

Overheating

Bright sunlight shining on translucent or dark material can lead to high temperatures. Keep plants in the shade, even when in bags or other containers. The co-extruded bags should not be covered with a non-reflective material, as this can cause them to heat up.

Physical damage

Broken roots or shoots are visible, but unseen internal damage from rough handling is just as important in reducing the vigour of planting stock. Never throw bags of plants around. Unload carefully. Do not stack other materials on top of plants. Do not use the spade to push roots into the ground.

PLATE 9 Plants being packaged into co-extruded bags directly after lifting in the nursery. It is essential that their roots do not dry out. (40268)

PLATE 10 If trees are left exposed before planting there is a risk of the roots being dried by the sun and wind. (*40269*)

PLATE 11 Careless handling of trees reduces their quality. (*40270*)

19

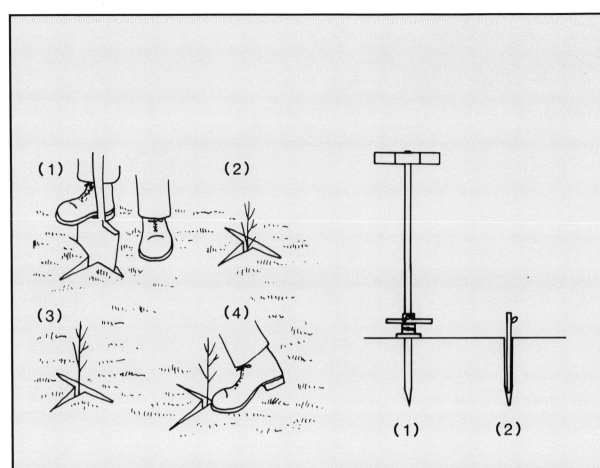

FIGURE 2 Planting transplants using the 'T' notch method.
1. Make plenty of room for the tree roots.
2. Ensure the tree roots are pushed as far down as possible.
3. Withdraw the transplant slightly to spread the roots.
4. Firm the ground gently with the ball of the foot to ensure good contact between the soil and the tree roots.

FIGURE 3 Planting unrooted cuttings of poplar and willow.
1. Using a suitable instrument, make a hole into which the cutting can be placed.
2. The cutting should be snug fit in the hole with 2–3 cm of the cutting above the soil surface to expose the uppermost bud.

Planting

Trees with bare roots should be planted using the notch planting method: it is suitable for all species. A spade is used to cut a 'T' or 'L' shaped slit in the ground. After making the second cut the spade is used to lever open the first slit and the roots of the tree are gently placed into the notch ensuring even distribution and no distortion of the roots. Firm the plant in using the ball of the foot. Ensure that the plant is left vertical and not bent to one side.

Unrooted cuttings of poplar and willow are planted by carefully inserting the cuttings into a hole made with a suitably sized bar leaving about 2–3 cm above the soil surface to expose the uppermost bud. The cuttings should be a snug fit in the hole and to prevent the cuttings being rocked by wind when they start to grow (but before the roots are firmly anchored) any surplus space within the hole should be packed with dry sand.

Time of planting

The normal planting season runs from late September to late March. However, early autumn planting is only possible if dormant stock can be obtained from the nursery. In seasons when the autumn is mild, trees do not become dormant until late in the year and the dispatching of plants from the nursery is delayed. Broadleaved trees in particular benefit from planting before the middle of November. Early spring planting, before any signs of flushing is usually successful but late spring plantings are vunerable if followed by a prolonged spring drought when losses can be high. Just as with agricultural crops the best establishment is achieved if planting takes place when soils are in optimum condition to allow cultivation. This is more important on sites with heavy soils (see 'Planting into an arable stubble' p.8–9).

Spacing/stocking density

When establishing trees on land which is coming out of intensive agriculture it is important to obtain an adequate stocking through planting because there will be little or no infilling from natural regeneration or coppice regrowth as is the case when a woodland site is replanted. The optimum stocking density will depend on the objectives of management and is most important for broadleaved trees, when the production of quality timber is a high priority. Planting at wide spacing makes it vitally important that every tree is successfully established and great attention must be paid to replacing failures. Planting fewer trees also leads to poorer choice when thinning, and because of the lack of competition between the trees they will usually have poorer stem form, i.e. be less straight and more heavily branched.

To grow quality timber, oak and beech (which have poor apical dominance) should not be planted at less than 3100 trees/ha and conifers and other broadleaved timber species, with the exception of cherry, at not less than 2500 trees/ha (see 'Mechanisation of operations'). Cherry has strong apical dominance and it is therefore acceptable to plant this species at 1100 trees/ha, but pruning will be necessary to prevent the development of low branches. Where amenity or conservation objectives are uppermost, a high stocking density is less important.

Protection

Newly planted trees need to be protected from rabbits, hares and deer. Where these animals are present the trees should be protected by either fencing or individual treeguards or treeshelters. As the size of the area increases above about 1 ha fencing will become proportionally less expensive than individual tree protection. The exact area above which fencing is cheaper depends on the shape of the area to be planted and the boundary length in relation to the number of trees planted. A properly erected fence has the advantage that it clearly defines the woodland area preventing trespass by farm stock or machinery. A fence and particularly a deer fence will also offer a greater degree of protection for many years longer than individual treeshelters.

On exposed sites treeshelters can cause serious damage to the stems of young trees when they emerge from the top of the treeshelters and the staking of trees may be necessary once the shelter has been degraded. In these situations a fence may be more effective and easier to maintain. However a fence will not protect the tree against damage from voles and as vole populations may increase rapidly (particularly where a grass sward is established between the trees) vole guards may be necessary in addition to a fence. Fences can be a disadvantage where woodlands are created for game cover as they prevent birds from easily entering and leaving the wood (see 'Game cover', pp.34–38). Treeshelters do allow easy application of foliar acting herbicides around the base of trees and if care is taken this operation can be mechanised.

On particularly weedy sites, even where a fence is used, there may be a case for protecting the trees with short treeshelters simply to allow the frequent use of relatively cheap foliar-acting herbicides to maintain effective weed control around the trees (see 'Species selection in relation to site factors, weed type and tree protection' p.29–30). The choice of what form of tree protection to use will depend on local circumstances and the objectives of woodland management.

PLATE 12 Oak emerging from treeshelters in the second growing season after planting. Treeshelters gradually degrade over a period of between 5 and 10 years. Note good weed control; essential for rapid tree establishment. (38057)

PLATE 13 A vole guard combined with a weed-free area gives a tree good protection. (*39251*)

PLATE 14 Mechanisation of mowing the inter-row vegetation. Residual herbicides were used to control weeds along the tree rows. (*40158*)

Mechanisation of operations

The maintenance of a newly planted woodland can be expensive and even impractical unless mechanisation is possible. If mechanisation is planned it is important to allow sufficient space between the trees and sufficiently large headlands to allow tractors or other equipment (i.e. farm bikes) to turn.

However, there can be conflict between planting to allow access to agricultural tractors and the production of quality timber which demands that the trees are planted at reasonably close spacing. If the primary objective is to produce high quality timber, then the options are either to plant trees at close spacing in the tree lines or to manage the inter-row vegetation by use of small horticultural machinery or the expanding range of equipment that is now available for use with four-wheel drive farm bikes.

5 Weed and vegetation management

Weed control

Experience gained by the Forestry Commission from some of the very first farm woodland experiments involving new planting revealed that *attention to weed control/vegetation management is the key to successful tree establishment on ex-agricultural sites.* Weeds reduce both the survival and growth of trees by competing for light, nutrients and most important of all, for moisture – particularly in low rainfall areas. Soil moisture deficits become greater under weeds than under bare soil because vegetation can lose moisture more rapidly and for a longer time before soil moisture potential limits transpiration. In comparison, relatively little moisture evaporates from bare soil before a layer of dry soil forms, restricting further moisture loss.

The majority of sites where trees are planted both in the uplands and in the lowlands benefit from weed control during the establishment phase. However, regularly cutting or mowing weeds, especially grass, is of no use since it increases their rate of water use by maintaining them in active growth, allowing them to compete more effectively and for longer during the growing season. The most cost-effective method of weed control is through the use of herbicides.

Control of weeds need not extend over the whole site in order to obtain improved survival and early growth of trees. Maintaining a weed-free area either as a 1 m² spot around the base of each tree or as a 1 m wide strip down the tree row will give very satisfactory results. Spot weeding is perfectly acceptable, but strip weeding allows mechanisation through the

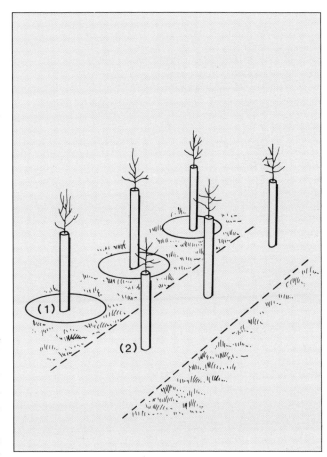

FIGURE 4 Methods of weed control.
1. Spot weeding, keeping 1 m² around the base of the tree weed free.
2. Strip weeding, keeping a 1 m wide band down the tree rows weed free. Strip weeding has the advantage that it can be mechanised.

use of adapted agricultural spraying equipment. Weed control is only essential during the establishment phase, normally for the first 3 years after planting.

Land managed for agricultural production usually has an enormous number of weed seeds in the soil. These are generally not apparent because, under pasture, grass prevents most weed species becoming established and under arable crops, weeds are controlled initially by herbicides and later by the smothering effect of the crop. Whether agricultural soils are left unmanaged or efforts are made to maintain bare ground, a succession of weed species takes place, although not disturbing a cereal stubble may delay and reduce this influx to some extent (see 'Previous land use' pp.6–9). This process starts with a rapid invasion of volunteers from the previous crop and annual arable weeds. Gradually these annual weeds are replaced by perennials many of which are deep rooting and difficult to remove selectively using herbicides between broadleaved trees and some conifers. Examples of such weeds are dandelion, docks, creeping thistle, perennial nettle and bramble. The best way to remove these weeds is by repeated application of foliar-acting herbicides, applied in ways which avoid contact with the trees.

Methods of weed control

As mentioned above we are only concerned with controlling the weeds in a 1 m diameter spot or a 1 m wide band along the tree rows. Mechanical control of weeds, by cultivation, in this area is not really an option because it has to be repeated frequently during the growing season, leaves the loose soil subject to erosion and can cause serious damage to tree roots. Therefore the most appropriate methods of controlling the weeds around the base of trees is through the use of mulches or herbicides.

PLATE 15 Strip weeding being practised in a newly planted farm woodland. (39604)

PLATE 16 A farm woodland site which received no weed control. (*38991*). The site has been invaded by weeds. The ground in the background was fully cultivated and has been invaded by broadleaved arable weeds, mostly groundsel. This weed was 2 metres tall. The ground in the foreground was a grass sward which was killed using herbicides, but not disturbed. This area has been invaded by various types of grass including wild oats and arable grass weeds.

The photograph demonstrates how pre-planting treatment of the site can dramatically affect the weed spectrum of an area.

Herbicides

The products can be divided into three broad groups:

1. **Residual herbicides.** These products act via the soil where they are taken up through the roots of weeds. It is important that these herbicides are applied to damp soil and that rain follows application to move them into the top 2–3 cm of the soil. If these products are applied to dry soil and little or no rainfall follows application, weed control will be poor. Residual herbicides must be applied to a firm fine tilth; if large clods are present at the time of herbicide application these will weather and crumble, exposing untreated soil allowing prolific weed growth.

2. **Foliar acting herbicides.** These are absorbed through the point of contact on the leaf and stem and are independent of the condition of the soil. The timing of application will be determined by the growth stage of the target weed. Foliar acting herbicides give best results when they are applied to actively growing weeds.

3. **Residual and foliar acting herbicides.** These are herbicides which have a combination of the two modes of action listed above. However, in practice, most of the herbicides in this group are biased towards either residual or foliar activity.

Depending on the susceptibility of the tree species, herbicides are applied as an overall spray (over the top of the trees and the weeds) or as a directed spray (placed to avoid contact with the trees). As a general rule do not apply herbicides, particularly selective foliar acting herbicides, as an overall application, during periods of bright sunlight or high temperatures as this can lead to scorching of tree foliage. If overall applications are needed in the summer then they should be made in the evening so there is the maximum period between application and the occurrence of high temperatures. Never apply herbicides of any description to waterlogged ground or when trees are under stress from drought.

Herbicides can be used effectively before or after planting. There may be opportunities to control perennial weeds in the previous crop, e.g. use of selective herbicides in pasture or the use of glyphosate pre-harvest in cereals and other arable crops. Such treatments can reduce the subsequent vigour of weeds such as creeping thistle or couch grass. Foliar-acting herbicides can be used to clean up undisturbed stubbles before planting.

Where long-term weed control is required after planting the use of residual herbicides is the best option. It is vital to match the weed control spectrum of the herbicide to that of the weed species on the site. Many residual herbicides generally only control weeds pre-emergence and must therefore be applied to bare earth. If bare soil is to be maintained all year round, treatment may be repeated in the autumn and the spring. However, in practice, weeds resistant to the residual herbicides being used begin to develop, and a regime based on foliar acting and residual herbicides (sometimes applied as a tank mixture) is needed. As an alternative to a year-round bare-soil system, some vegetation cover may be allowed to develop in the autumn and winter when it is not competitive and then be killed by a spring applied foliar-acting herbicide. A spring applied residual treatment will then delay reinvasion.

The herbicides used to control weed growth in farm woodlands will be some of those used in conventional agriculture because the same weed spectrum is present. Forestry Commission research is currently testing agricultural herbicides to identify those which are tolerated by a wide range of tree species. Forestry Commission Research Information Note 201 gives specific recommendations for the use of herbicides in farm woodlands.

Mulches

Organic mulches can be provided by growing a cover crop such as rye-grass or cereals, then killing the cover with a foliar acting herbicide before or after tree planting. Applications of a thick layer of organic material such as wood chips or straw after planting can suppress weeds but such mulches are difficult to keep in place and their use may lead to a reduction in tree growth, since much available nitrogen is used for microbial breakdown of the mulch. Perennial weeds eventually grow through these mulches and have to be controlled by herbicides.

Various forms of synthetic mulch have been used including black polythene mulch mats (1 × 1 m) and the same material applied as a 1 m wide strip. These impervious mulches have the advantage of retaining soil moisture normally lost by evaporation from bare soil and are particularly useful on very light soils. They may last 3–4 years. There is some evidence that plastic film may lead to reduced growth on poorly drained soils due to the formation of anaerobic conditions beneath the sheet. Plastic film can be damaged by perennial weeds and rooks. It can also provide sheltered conditions for voles which can then debark trees from beneath the mulch. Foxes will rip the plastic material when in pursuit of voles. The high cost of purchasing and laying mulches is a disadvantage.

Species selection in relation to site factors, weed type and tree protection

Ideally the sites selected for planting trees on farms should be free of perennial weeds that will cause problems during the establishment period. In practice however, sites are generally chosen for other reasons. Assuming factors other than the presence of weeds take priority in site choice, weed control should influence decisions on what tree species are grown and on tree protection.

On sites heavily infested with perennial weeds successful tree establishment will be much easier to achieve where weeds that develop can be treated with foliar-acting herbicides, some of which may be non-selective. Thus, tree species that are tolerant of overall sprays of foliar-acting herbicides (i.e. pines and spruces which will tolerate overall sprays of glyphosate in the autumn when they are dormant) or trees protected by short or tall treeshelters would be a viable option, whereas susceptible trees without individual protection (within a fenced area) would not. So, if safe spraying with foliar-acting herbicides is not possible, susceptible unprotected trees should not be planted on sites heavily infested with perennial weeds.

Sites with very variable soil texture and depth can cause problems in weed control because the performance of residual herbicides is affected. These treatments may cause damage on sandy/gravelly patches due to increased herbicide leaching. In areas where the soil is compacted, root penetration will be restricted and trees may take up damaging amounts of herbicide from the surface layers. In such situations residual herbicide treatments with a high tolerance margin should be used or only foliar-acting herbicides applied. Soils with a high pH can increase the availability of some soil acting herbicides and can cause problems where tree tolerance is marginal.

Steep slopes present problems with residual herbicides if they are prone to soil erosion. Erosion of soil treated with a soil acting herbicide may lead to inadequate dose on the slope, a build up of residue where the soil is deposited, or loss in surface runoff. In situations where soil is loose, residual herbicides are best avoided.

The factors listed above which affect weed occurrence and control are unlikely to influence the decision on whether to plant trees on a particular site but they should affect decisions on the species of tree to plant, tree protection and the weed control system. Without consideration of these factors at the planning stage, expensive and unsightly failures will occur.

Decision steps for weed control around trees

Planning an appropriate and effective weed control programme can be helped by systematically working through the objectives of the planting, the problems anticipated and the preferred methods. This can be done by completing a specifications form (see page 36). When this background information has been recorded, detailed planning of the programme can take place.

The next stage involves the choice of treatments. With mulches the decision may be based on the choice of cover crop to be grown before being killed with a herbicide to act as an organic mulch over the whole site. Or if mulching is to take place around individual trees or down the planted row the decision may be based on the availability of materials (organic or synthetic), machinery and labour and the weed types present.

If herbicides are to be used then the choice of herbicides will depend on factors such as tree species to be planted, weeds present, the level of control required and herbicide cost. Mixtures of residual herbicides are often necessary when a broad weed spectrum is to be controlled. When considering the weed population it is important to establish which species are perennial and difficult to control and which will need to be treated with a foliar-acting herbicide. Costs can often be reduced by localised treatments with foliar-acting herbicides rather than treating the whole area; this will often be the case for follow-up treatments in the summer on patches of perennial weeds.

PLATE 17 1 m² mulch mats in use on a farm woodland.

PLATE 18 A normal agricultural sprayer adapted by the addition of a short boom on the rear of the sprayer for use in farm woodlands. (40156)

Vegetation management in the inter-row

Between the spots or strips which must be kept weed free to achieve good survival and early growth of the trees there is an area of ground which, if left unmanaged, will develop prolific weed growth. On the heaviest of soils this area may have to be kept more or less bare for the first year after planting to avoid the problems associated with uneven shrinkage of the soil (see 'Soil type: physical properties' p.10). On many sites it is surprisingly difficult to maintain bare ground as a succession of weeds exploit the vacant space. The use of residual herbicides can control most of the annual arable weeds but annual and particularly perennial weeds that are unaffected by these herbicides quickly take advantage of the lack of competition (see 'Weed control' p.25).

On most sites it is much preferable to have some form of ground vegetation present. Techniques that maintain vegetation in the inter-row avoid the expensive and unsightly practice of trying to maintain bare ground with the associated problems of high herbicide input, soil erosion and nitrate leaching.

There are two basic approaches to maintain good weed control for the promotion of rapid tree establishment and the management of ground flora in the inter-row:

1. Impose weed control around the planted trees and accept whatever vegetation develops on the site between the weed free areas.

2. Impose weed control around the planted trees and sow a ground cover crop between the weed-free areas. The sown crop may also have uses other than simply weed suppression, e.g. game cover.

Whichever approach is chosen it is essential that the ground vegetation is managed. Hence the need to have access to the site during the growing season (see 'Accessibility' p.6). It is for this reason that many farm woodlands are laid out to allow access with small agricultural tractors between the tree rows (see 'Mechanisation of operations' p.24).

Managing naturally occurring vegetation

If naturally occurring vegetation is accepted in the inter-row then it should be managed by regular mowing to prevent it seeding and becoming a recurring problem and a source of weed seed which can spread into neighbouring crops. Frequent passes with the mower will be necessary to achieve this aim because once weeds have become established some species can produce new seed heads as quickly as 10 days after being cut. However, mowing is a quick and relatively cheap operation when mechanised.

Sowing inter-row vegetation

The second approach is to introduce vegetation into the inter-row. This can be used simply to exclude the weeds or it can fulfil other objectives such as game cover, in addition to the establishment of woodland. Whatever vegetation is chosen it should have a low productivity. This not only reduces the cost of management but will also reduce the extraction of moisture which can lead to problems of uneven shrinkage particularly on heavy soils (see 'Weed control' p.25) and adverse competition with the trees. It is therefore important to choose a species that can be selectively removed from the base of the trees. Clover is very competitive for moisture and is difficult to remove from around trees and should therefore not be used.

If the suppression of weeds is the sole aim of inter-row vegetation then the simplest solution is a

PLATE 19 Heavy soil kept weed free during the first growing season, using residual herbicides to avoid the problems associated with uneven soil shrinkage. (*39621*)

PLATE 20 The naturally occurring vegetation, which on this site is predominantly redshank, has been mown to prevent it seeding and becoming an annual problem. Although the redshank has grown over the weed free strip it has not rooted into the herbicide treated soil. (*39610*)

PLATE 21 An area where no weed control or management of the naturally occurring vegetation (redshank) in the inter-row vegetation has taken place. This site will act as a source of seeds which will infest neighbouring fields. A lack of weed control will result in high tree mortality and poor growth of the trees which survive. (*39613*)

grass sward. This can be sown over the whole site before the trees are planted and then removed from around the base of the trees with herbicides (see 'Weed control' pp.25–26) or it can be sown between the weed free areas (in the inter-row) after planting. Low productivity species such as fescues are a good choice.

Game cover

Another option, which enables the weeds to be controlled between the weed-free areas and fulfils another objective, is to establish a game cover crop in the inter-row. This technique was pioneered by the Game Conservancy and it allows newly established woodland to enhance the value of a shooting enterprise within 1 year of planting. There are a number of possible crops which can be used but the one which has been used most successfully to date is kale. It is important to select a hardy variety, which should be sown in rows 50–60 cm apart in the June/July following tree planting. The ground in the inter-row must be kept clean before the kale is sown to allow the production of a seed bed, and normal pre-emergent weed control must be exercised on the area sown with kale.

Stock must be excluded as they will trample and eat the kale, and in severe winter weather pigeons may have to be controlled to prevent unacceptable damage. One way of excluding farm stock but allow-

PLATE 22 Kale drilled on 35 cm rows in June of the first growing season. Note weed-free strips down the tree rows. (39616)

PLATE 23 The same site as shown in Plate 22 in October of the first growing season. The kale is providing cover for pheasants. (39926)

PLATE 24 Grass/wild flower mixtures can be an extremely attractive feature within farm woodlands. (*Willmot Industries*)

Example of planning form 1: Factors which affect weed control options

Tree protection against foliar-acting herbicides — Tick boxes as appropriate

- Treeshelters ☐
- None ☐

Planting date
- Autumn ☐
- Spring ☐

State of ground
- Pasture ☐
- Uncultivated stubble ☐
- Cultivated ground ☐

Land preparation
- Plough and cultivate ☐
- Sub-soiling ☐
- None ☐

Main weed species anticipated
- Annual ☐
- Perennial — Broadleaf ☐
- Grasses ☐
- Mixed ☐

Distribution
- Overall ☐
- Patches ☐

Wood density — Tick boxes as appropriate
- Heavy ☐
- Moderate ☐
- Light ☐

Weed control method

Herbicides only
- Foliar-acting (FAH) only ☐
- Residual (RH) + foliar (FAH) ☐

No herbicide
- Mulch ☐
- Killed cover crop ☐
- Organic material ☐
- Plastic film ☐

Inter-row management
- Mow volunteer vegetation ☐

Establish inter-row cover
- Grass ☐
- Grass/wild flowers ☐
- Game cover crop ☐
- Other ☐

Example of planning form 2: Planning schedule for weed management

Specification

Shelters?	Yes	*Planting date?*	Spring
State of ground?	Stubble	*Land preparation?*	Plough
Control method?	Herbicides only	*Weed type?*	Annual + perennial

Weed species?	Creeping thistle, knotgrass, fat-hen, annual grass
Distribution?	Overall
Density?	Moderate

Treatment selection

Date	Weeding operation	Requirement	Date	Weeding operation	Requirement
Year 0			*Year 2*		
Jul/Aug	Spray previous crop FAH	*	Feb/Mar	Re-apply mulch	
Jul/Aug	Spray fallow FAH		Feb/Mar	Spray RH	
Aug/Sep	Plough	*	Feb/Mar	Spray FAH	
Sep	Cultivate	*	Feb/Mar	Spray RH + FAH	*
Sep	Sow cover-crop	*	Jun	Hoe/cut weeds	
			Jun/Jul	Spray summer FAH	*
Year 1			Sep/Oct	Spray RH	
Feb/Mar	Spray to kill cover-crop FAH		Sep/Oct	Spray FAH	
Feb/Mar	Spray weed growth FAH		Sep/Oct	Spray RH + FAH	*
Feb/Mar	PLANT TREES	*			
Feb/Mar	Apply mulch		*Year 3*		
Feb/Mar	Spray RH		Feb/Mar	Re-apply mulch	
Feb/Mar	Spray FAH		Feb/Mar	Spray RH	
Feb/Mar	Spray RH + FAH	*	Feb/Mar	Spray FAH	
Jun	Hoe/cut weeds		Feb/Mar	Spray RH + FAH	*
Jun/Jul	Spray follow-up FAH	*	Jun	Hoe/cut weeds	
Sep/Oct	Spray RH		Jun/Jul	Spray summer FAH	*
Sep/Oct	Spray FAH		Sep/Oct	Spray RH	
Sep/Oct	Spray RH + FAH	*	Sep/Oct	Spray FAH	
			Sep/Oct	Spray RH + FAH	*

RH, residual herbicide; FAH, foliar acting herbicide

ing game birds access to the woodland is to erect stock netting (with the specification C8/80/15 or C6/90/30) upside down. This will exclude all farm animals except small lambs but allow game birds to walk through the holes in the netting.

Following establishment, the kale requires very little management and remains useful for harbouring game birds for about 3 years. Seed produced by the kale can also provide a valuable winter food source for small birds, while the crop also provides shelter. Due to the tall dense canopy provided by the kale it effectively prevents most weeds from establishing and on exposed sites can nurse trees, protecting them from climatic extremes. A tall game cover crop also provides protection for treeshelters on exposed sites.

Wildlife benefits

A mixture of low productivity grasses and wild flowers can provide substantial wildlife benefits. The mixture can be sown before or after tree planting. The cost of the grass/wild flower mixture depends on the number of species included and the relative cost of the different species; seed merchants can provide different mixtures to suit most budgets. For optimum results it is essential to match the species of grass and wild flowers to the soil type of the area to be sown. Mixtures of grasses and herbs are attractive and the flower and seed heads will encourage and support many species of insects and birds. Such techniques can quickly transform the wildlife value of an area that was previously under intensive arable production.

Although probably too expensive to consider for large areas the establishment of a grass/wild flower sward is ideally suited to sheltered woodland edges and rides for the improvement of wildlife habitats, and adjacent to footpaths and bridleways for amenity and recreation benefits. The interest created by these techniques will only last until the tree canopy closes, but interest can be sustained as successive areas are planted. The wildlife value of any wood is dynamic and will change as the woodland structure develops.

PLATE 25 Where the inter-row is sown with a grass/wild flower mixture it is attractive in the autumn and effectively excludes weeds. (39925)

6   Establishing woodland for conservation

Planning the woodland

The conversion of farmland to woodland will almost certainly bring wildlife benefits, but these can be very greatly improved by careful planning. The open spaces within woodlands often provide a diversity of habitats which support a wide variety of wildlife. During the initial stages of establishment nearly all the area can be thought of as open-space and species diversity can be increased very quickly (see 'Vegetation management in the inter-row' p.32). However, when planning the new woodland provision should be made for a network of permanent rides and glades. These will provide habitats for wildlife associated with woodland edges and open-spaces once the trees have begun to dominate the site.

Often the provision of such facilities can aid other management objectives. Wide rides are not only better for butterflies, but they are also drier and therefore allow easier access for woodland operations and they improve the potential of a wood for pheasant shooting. However, wide rides can adversely affect the sheltered conditions favoured by some woodland species, notably insects. The creation of curved rides, with shelter provided by allowing a scatter of trees in places, will help to decrease wind speed.

Ride mowing can increase the diversity of the ground flora and the density of plant cover within the wood, particularly those requiring periodic light conditions such as violet, primrose, wood anemone, greater stitchwort and lesser celandine. The frequency and timing of mowing depends on local conditions and on the plants and animals for which the site is being managed. Wherever possible cuttings should be removed to avoid desirable plants being lost under a mulch of cut material and to reduce the risk of nutrient enrichment.

Shrubs and trees should be cut every 3–7 years during the dormant period to avoid disturbing nesting birds and feeding insects. Grass and broadleaved herbaceous plants should be cut every 2–5 years, but exact timing of the cut is less clear. Cutting from October onwards has been advocated in the past as it was thought to have least effect on invertebrate populations. However, there is now evidence that cutting during the non-growing season may encourage a few vigorous grasses to dominate, leading to a severe reduction in plant diversity. This may be a greater problem in new woodlands on former agricultural land, where soils may well be deeper and more fertile. Summer cutting of a proportion of the area may maintain a herb-rich sward in the long term without a significant reduction in invertebrate populations.

Rides should not be cut uniformly. Scalloped or bay shapes can be formed instead, these will reduce the wind-tunnel effect particularly on long straight rides and increase visual variety.

The amount of management that is required in different types of non-woodland habitat can vary greatly and will depend on the type of habitat and the specific objectives of management. With wet marshy areas a low or non-intervention policy is usually the best option. But there will need to be active management if glades are to be kept open.

Further reading

Forestry Commission Publications

Bulletins

62   Silviculture of broadleaved woodland
66   Choice of seed origins for the main forest species in Britain
75   The silviculture and yield of wild cherry
80   Farm woodland planning
91   The timbers of farm woodland trees
92   Poplars for wood production and amenity
102 Forest fencing
105 Roe deer biology and management
106 Woodland management for pheasants

Booklets

15   Conifers
20   Broadleaves

Handbooks

2   Trees and weeds: weed control for successful tree establishment
3   Farm woodland practice
6   Forestry practice
7   Treeshelters
9   Growing broadleaves for quality timber

Field Book

8   The use of herbicides in the forest

Guidelines

Forests and water guidelines
Forest landscape design guidelines
Lowland landscape design guidelines
Forest nature conservation guidelines

Occasional Papers

14   The Gwent Small Woods Project 1979–1984
17   Farming and forestry

Forest Record

124 The fallow deer

Research Information Notes

126 Enhancement of lowland forest ridesides and roadsides to benefit wild plants and butterflies
155 Farm forestry research
156 Demonstration plots for farm woodland and amenity tree establishment
170 A brief guide to some aspects of the Pesticide Regulations 1986
181 The introduction of improved poplar clones from Belgium
201 Herbicides for farm woodlands and short rotation coppice

Arboricultural Research Notes

8/79/ARB   Damage to broadleaved seedlings by desiccation
22/80/ARB   Root deformation by biodegradable containers
27/88/SILS   Herbicides for sward control among broadleaved amenity trees
29/81/SILS   The native and exotic trees in Britain
40/89/ARB   Tree staking
53/90/WS   Chemical weeding: hand held direct applicators

59/89/ARB	The effect of weed competition on tree establishment
63/87/SILS	Treeshelters
67/87/ARB	A comparison of the survival and growth of transplants, whips and standards, with and without weeding
69/87/SILS	Do soil ameliorants help tree establishment?
71/87/ARB	Black polythene mulches to aid tree establishment
72/87/ARB	Sheet mulches: suitable materials and how to use them
74/90/ARB	Protecting trees from field voles

Miscellaneous

Practical work in farm woods. ADAS Leaflets P3160–P3167, MAFF/FC
Successful tree establishment

Other publications

BARNETT, P. (1988). *Shelter in the lowlands.* Leaflet P3187. MAFF/ADAS.

BECKETT, K. and BECKETT, G. (1979). *Planting native trees and shrubs.* Jarrold, Norwich.

BLYTH, J., EVANS, J., MUTCH, W.E.S. and SIDWELL, C. (1991). *Farm woodland management* (2nd edn). Farming Press, Ipswich.

BROOKS, A. (1980). *Woodlands – a practical conservation handbook.* British Trust for Conservation Volunteers, Wallingford.

GAME CONSERVANCY (1988). *Woodlands for pheasants.* Game Conservancy Booklet 15. Game Conservancy, Fordingbridge.

SMART, N. and ANDREWS, J. (1985). *Birds and broadleaves handbook.* Royal Society for the Protection of Birds, Sandy, Beds.

Printed in the United Kingdom for HMSO
Dd 293238 6/92 C35